MR. GOODMAN

AND

OTHER POEMS

By

Benedict Nnolim

First published 1993
by
CECTA (NIG.) LIMITED
ISBN 978-2396-05-2

Paperback, Second, edition, published 2008
ISBN 978-1-906914-14-1

Hardback edition published 2011
ISBN 978-1-906914-68-4

Other Books of Poetry by Ben Nnolim Books

Title	Paperback	Hardback	Lulu eBook
Mr Goodman and Other Poems	978-1-906914-14-1	978-1-906914-68-4	978-1-906914-32-5
Dialogue	978-1-906914-03-5	978-1-906914-57-8	978-1-906914-29-5
Graffiti	978-1-906914-07-3	978-1-906914-58-5	978-1-906914-31-8
They sold Us Mud	978-1-906914-53-0	978-1-906914-67-7	978-1-906914-50-9

Ben Nnolim Books.
3 Bekesbourne Tower,
Wichling Close,
Orpington, Kent. BR5 4QL
Email: benedictnnolim@aol.com

PREFACE TO THE FIRST PAPERBACK EDITION

Growing up, in one's cultural environment, can be a strenuous exercise. To grow up in another cultural environment, such as the cities of Western Europe provide, can be traumatic.

Many young Africans, who went to study overseas in the 60s, were subjected to a lot of tension - social, cultural, moral, technological and psychological.

This book is a collection of writings, in free verse, written in reaction to these tensions.

It will not be true to state that any piece, in this book, relates, exactly, to particular events and persons. What is true is that particular events and persons inspired, almost, all the pieces. To these persons, I am grateful.

I wish to thank my father, Mr. S. A. Nnolim (RIP), who introduced me, very early in life, to the power of knowledge, acquired by reading widely above one's level and within and outside one's main occupation and, then Mr., now Professor, Charles Nnolim who, during my primary school days, regaled me with highlights, and the beauty, of the books he had read or I was reading.

I wish to acknowledge, gratefully, the efforts of Theresa Nnaji, Christine Akiti and Mrs. Catherine Nwadioke, who typed the various versions of the manuscript.

Above all, I thank God for everything.

Benedict Nnolim
1993.

FOREWORD TO THE FIRST PAPERBACK EDITION

Poetry is the record of the private feelings of a sensitive soul in moments of elation, of a sudden but penetrating insight or of sheer sadness. The poems in this collection have, in them, more of sadness than elation, and may contradict Shelley's dictum that "poetry is the record of the best and happiest moments, of the best and happiest minds". The sum total of **Mr. Goodman and Other Poems**, by Ben Nnolim, tilts more towards Milton's **Il Penseroso** (the man of melancholy and pensive meditation) than to his **L'Allegro** (the man of heart-easing gaiety).

The poems, in this volume, record the journey of many young Nigerians (as can be glimpsed in the volume's major divisions **BEFORE, DURING, AFTER**) both *physical* and *psychological*: *physically* from the restricted environment of Nigeria to Great Britain and the United States; and *psychologically* from the gaiety and innocence of childhood (see "*African Innocence*") when with other children the poet "sang and danced so pure and free"; to a more mature man (see " *Sobering Thoughts*") where he stopped to observe that "things are not/what they seem, it's only play". The landscape of Mr. Goodman and Other Poems is replete with various aspects of human relationships--their loves, their hypocrisies, their insincerities, their gossips, their infidelities. Behind all these stands the poet who watches with cynicism and with a sneer - blended alarm at people's morals and sense of justice and fairness, himself untouched. One, standing apart or rather aloof with the poet's persona, can easily trace with him the contours of the landscape of his poetry as they refract on the poet's emotions, his sensitivities and his withdrawing revulsion from the kind of persons he is forced to get involved with, until he slaps himself to awaken ness with "*Grow Up*" which is one of his bitterest pieces, as he cynically loses faith in everything around him:

> Faith? Ha! Ha! Look again.
> Wh keeps it must want to die.
> Love? Ha! Ha! Come again…
> Morals? Ha! Justice? Boo!
> Caring? That's for fools…
> Chastity? Boy, you're green.

The poet's encounter with racism reach bothering proportions in "*Bigots*" where he seethes with suppressed anger at racists:

> All the smarting we suppress
> All the wrath and passion boiled
> All are stirred and stoked by them.

Of human beings in general, the poet seems to ask with Hamlet: "What is this quintessence of dust?: man delights not me: no, nor woman neither, though by your smiling you seem to say so" (Act II, Scene ii, lines 321 - 323): so that in " *A Girl I know*" he encounters a girl who has so perfected the art of telling lies that while she "tells me lies" she manages to "look so hard I change my gaze".

But the poet does not seem to spare himself as we find in his love relationships. Not for him the easy kill as he predictably encounters love situations that present not-so-easy solutions. In "*Khetiwe*" he weeps:

> What hearts have loved
> And souls despaired
> As much as you and I
> That safety which you seek
> I've dared
> Care not for it say I

And he concludes with "Normal paths give not much gain/In this terrain we have our love". But Khetiwe is neither the first nor the last foreign girl he met: he regrets in "*Foreign Charm*" that the fear which in retrospect he discovers was "in vain" had prevented him from marrying a foreign girl when "in chance we met our love" as he now, with hindsight, discovers

> Now I find my fears in vain
> Now in years I look again.
> I see your smile and lovely face
> And wish that I had had the grace.

Wasn't it D. H. Lawrence who says that one sheds one's sickness in books; or as some other writers with a tragic cast of mind might put it, one sings a song to relieve an aching heart. **Mr. Goodman and Other Poems**, as I hinted earlier, is a spiritual autobiography revealing the philosophic pessimism of a sensitive mind who does not find life's game funny in the least. The collection, characteristically, opens with "*Futility*" and predictably ends on a sad note with the very last poem "*Knife Edge Friends*" where the poet's seeming friends are all smiling villains who are more dangerous than sharp two-edged knives. The poet would

> ... Rather take the knives
> Than have these friends that fill your stock
> Who breathe and talk but cut like knives

Finally, the title poem of the collection, "*Mr. Goodman*" deserves special attention as the centre piece of the foregoing discussion. In it the poet's persona laments his lot in life, wondering why "I labour not to hurt/But they hurt me/All the time": and why in the minds of malicious gossips

"Nothing is ever strange/That I cannot do". It worries him no end that "I offer the whole of me/Thinking, in friendliness/But I reap resentment". He is a much-misunderstood man who wonders in bewilderment why others are understood if they say they are sick or broke or have problems but not he. And he frets that with this attitude, were he to be dead, his friends would still expect him to rise from the dead to attend first to their needs. He ends it thus:

> See? Don't you? It's all my fault.
> I'm not a good man, not at all

But in spite of the various serious facts of life recorded by the poet in this volume, he took time out to write poems "in the lighter mood", the kind of poems Wordsworth tells us are "thoughts recollected in tranquility" (see "*For a Walk*", "*Life in Full*", "*Respite*"). Satiric pieces also abound (see "*The Right Approach*" or "*An Army Man*"). these are not mere diversions from the seriousness of his themes which transcend personal experiences to embrace the present world order in a social milieu that has gone berserk with loose morality (see "*Evil in Town*" and "*Empowered Girl*"), and general insincerity among otherwise enlightened men and women. No, they are part of the poet's world view which takes in its sweep the good, and the ugly, while insisting that the poet is confused as he watches those around him flouting all the rules we were taught to live by and seeming to enjoy it.

Poets are born, not made. In this collection, Mr. Ben Nnolim, a Chemical Engineer by training, may have, unwittingly, struck gold mines of philosophic speculations in an age of the fast Naira and mundane pursuits of the false symbols of life by a majority of the Nigerian populace. Comedy, it is said, is the product of a mind that feels, while tragedy is the product of a mind which thinks. ***Mr. Goodman and Other Poems*** teases us out of thought. I urge it on the reading public as a new voice in the landscape of Nigerian poetry.

Charles E. Nnolim
Professor of English,
University of Port Harcourt.

PREFACE TO THIS EDITION

The generation of Nigerians, who came to Europe and the Americas in the 1960s, is quite different from those who now migrate from Nigeria to Europe and the Americas. That generation, whether it liked it or not, was more concerned with the then prevalence, in Nigeria, of the so-called colonial mentality, with the imperative to be free from it and with the urge to express an authentic African identity, than the present generation of Nigerian emigrants who care less about these issues and more about their personal, economic, situation.

The 1960's Europe and Nigeria were quite different from today's Europe and Nigeria. Nigeria of the 1960s was hopeful and sought national and racial liberation while in the Europe, of the same period, its youth, confident of itself, sought individual liberty and a rejection of their parents' colonial or imperial past.

The cultural stress and strain endured by Nigerians living in Europe, of today, have decreased or at least have changed in character. It is living in Nigeria of today that has become more stressful and strenuous than in the 1960s because the hopes and aspirations of the 1960s have become not only mirages but, in fact, nightmares, leading to mass exodus of youths in search of relief and security abroad (see the poem Just My Life (Brain Drain?))

Social structure and morality in Nigeria have, since, collapsed. The nationalism of the 1960s has descended into self-destructive, blind, and thoughtless individualism using tribalism, euphemistically labelled ethnicity, as a dishonest excuse to pursue individualistic goals.

This book is not an attempt to recommend solutions to these problems. It is merely a record of the perspectives of one person who has lived through these experiences. Good reading.

Benedict Nnolim
December 4, 2011.

Table of Contents

BEFORE

FUTILITY

When I'm sad and lonely bound
I wish I had some happy sound.
When I'm glad and happy so,
I fear that lonesome I may go.

Must we live our lives like this?
Are there other ways?
Must we fret and pine away,
dreaming, doubting, seeking peace?

All are born and try to live
in this tender-hardy place.
This we do not quite relate
as we try and fight to live.

TO GET ON

This world of ours I lay my bet,
a happy, jolly, place.
What you want, you, likely, get
if you keep the pace.

Is it joy and pleasure's tent?
Be yourself, your mind's ferment.
Is it love or heart's content?
Make your feet and hands contend.

AFRICAN INNOCENCE

Those moonlit nights, the good old days!
A child I was but then, I saw.
Such a beauty for my days.
Nature bared; it was thawed.
We, always, supped and then, we played.
A custom old but grand and rare.

We, often, ran and chased ourselves,
and dashed, carefree, across the farms.
We feared the thorns but ran amok.
We, sometimes, fell and got a shock.

Around was nature, like a glen,
When, with moonlight, it was blend.
The walls you knew that they were red.
The leaves, you're sure, were all in green.
The sandy paths you used to tread,
now, in colours strange were formed

It was grand, yes, when you danced.
You sang and danced, so pure and free,
from song to chant and chant to song.
Boys and girls, by arms, were fenced.
Your bodies touched, you did not think
of male or female or such things.

Often, two will come and dance,
while, in joy, you chorus clapped.
Thus, we lived and played our lives,
not knowing what they know today.

FOR A WALK

The wind has, truly, got my heart.
In wonder, new, I'm born.
This must be the moon I've known,
the air, the skies, the earth.

So soft and tender in these lights,
so cool and fresh the airs.
Your eves, Nsukka, in July,
your eves a joy to ply.

Alone, I, really, thought I was.
So full of worries, I was sure.
Now, I know how blind I was
in your presence and your love.

Oh my gosh! I see things new!
With fairy joys I gloat.
Who knows when all these will be loathe,
or when I look and cannot see?

The call is far and that to me.
The air is better over there.
My tired legs have, now, some strength
For me to spend to roam.

The head is light, I feel it well.
My limbs are lithe, it's not just talk.
The lust, perhaps, of tramps I smell
I say I want a walk.

VANITY

I stop and wonder, much, sometimes,
at things that, long, have been around.
How, with time, they do not fret
as much as man and haste.

The trees, in wind and violent rain.
will bear their leaves and fruits terrain.
In gusts of wind they bend and bend,
to keep their stand on mother earth.

The lands are there and not in vain.
They feed us all with the help of rain.
The grass does thrive, and all things born,
even mud, sand, and rock.

We all must die and turn to dust
whether or not we like the thought.
Yet we fight without a thought
over money, land, or love.

When you fight to own the land,
or rush to court to win your case,
spinning tales and lies to win,
can you spend some time to think?

Why not think of those two goats
on a narrow mountain pass?
Willing not to let it pass,
they lost their lives as foolish goats.

While they humped and while they charged

on the narrow mountain pass,
all around in quiet peace,
stood the mountains fast asleep!

SOBERING THOUGHT

When, with joy, in glee, I soar;
when my heart to heaven's oars,
I, often, stop to think of times
when things were not as, now, they are.

How the people move and play.
How, in bliss, they dance for joy.
Will they know it, things are not
what they seem, it's, only, play.

DURING

IS THIS ME?

If this is me, then let me in
if, by your ways, I fall into the pit.
Our created natures, unblemished, excellent,
are aimed at when they are of the soul's essence.
Which no toil or sorrows can hurt.
And its virtues, like flaming swords of Eden, cut.
If the forest of undergrowth and overgrowth unending,
which, though our eyes peep and necks are bending,
block the skies, the stars, the moon, even the sun's light.
That, now, confused, we cannot see nor seek aright,
and lose our base on which our life is right.
Then what is me? Give me Me.
And take the prize and leave me behind.

MISSION CHILD

The wisdom of their ways has won.
And the follies of the "honest" pine for joy.
The trusting heart, well deceived in time,
cannot abide finesse or openness of mind.
It can give. It can take. But did not care
to put the feelings in their proper place.
There are fantasies of childhood and the aspiring to
Heaven. The inexperience, the credulity, of the days,
were unleavened. There were agents of Heaven and, of
course, this obliging heart. The wonders of this knife, so
blunt, yet much in need, against the coarsest and
smoothest stones ground, cannot be honed. And each
effort, each drop of water, takes its toll of sweat,
that turn to tears at the unmercifulness and sight of death
And the effort of will, its magic gone, withers in fear,

11

absconding from the paths of Faith

LIFE IN FULL

Oh! The beauty of these things!
Now, in peace, I stare, surprised.
Full of wonder, how so wise,
we cheat ourselves of Heaven things.

See the bright and beautiful sun,
shining, dazzling, bright, all day!
Or the silvery moon at night,
bright and queenly, gone so gay.

Can you touch and feel how soft,
darkness, hazy, black, can be?
Are there loving eyes for you
to trust and warm the empty you?

When the tales of triumph thrill,
and reins of duty help to hone
talents of your treasure trove,
search no more for other thrills.

But thank your God
and thank Him well.
For what you have
is life in full.

WHITE AFRICAN

See the Been-to, fresh from school,
how, with zeal and fervour White,

caring not, he looks with scorn,
on things that come and do with Blacks.

Most of them would like, in truth,
to make their Dead as proud as trees.
Yes, they try but, often, fail.
Who can Nature's ways escape?

How can he and when you wish
break the bonds they've put on him?
He was born and ate their meals.
All your ways are new to him.

It is chick to claim a root.
Heritage, ancestral roots.
What a root for Africans!
Starving children, despots, coups.
What is there to brag about?

They have this trait, it is from birth.
I have to say it loud and clear.
They show it every time they can.
It is a trait they shouldn't have.
whether they've been to or they've not.

Though they're safe in Western lands,
where the rule is give and take,
to everyone their earthly stake.
Not the Been-to African,
power is his, so yield or die.

Their sight of fellow Africans
lends them speech and acts so clear;

that brothers, sisters, African,
are black as Black and not their type.

You would think the deals they get,
discrimination, racial stress,
would make them see and know their kind.
And ease their burdens with a smile

Alas! They're White and African
Born, with glee, to spite their kind.

PEACE IS GONE

The ways of peace are gone.
And the agonies of war cannot be borne.
Let us will and aim not to cry,
our strength will not let us try.
That so, we console ourselves, my friends,
with forgetfulness and other exciting trends.
And our powers of judgment and good sense,
lose and destroy themselves in this sequence
which, if by pain and diligence, we remove
makes way for others that suit the mood.

REGRETS

There's a beauty in these things,
in this, eventual, nothingness.
A busyness I find exciting
even when it has no point.

We vanquish all the fears we have.
And pride ourselves that we have won.

What kind of soldiers go to fight?
Or rush to war in armour torn?

See the peace that's so sublime.
See the joy that's out of time.
We make our fronts to look perfect
to show that we can stand the siege.

The wall surrounds us in a try
when with prudence we will toy.
In time, on us appears a shroud
that shields and hides a cloud.

Hopeful, brave and now in charge
we leap and dash to make our mark,
with our strength our well of fear,

And plans, in dreams, and past despair,
we took as history not as hope
heap on us some great regrets
when we crash with them on us.

RESPITE

The moon was out and shone so gay.
The breeze was there and felt so fresh.
The trees did dance, they waved at me.
My windowpane I saw alive.

I heard it sing. I saw it dance.
I saw it move with the evening breeze.
The blinds were shuffling, heaved as well,
slow but graceful to his tune.

15

The stars had shirked their flight to watch
and brought a light to mend my heart.

KHETIWE

What hearts have loved and souls despaired
as much as you and I?
That safety which you seek I've dared.
Care not for it, say I.

If two there were so much alike,
then, for us, there's not a need.
In pain, in years, we sought for right,
so, cannot stand with sagging knees.

What fear had we that came to ride?
And all, to you, is new again.
Let them gloat in tattered joy.
Normal paths give not much gain.

In this terrain we have our love
and this is more than gain.

HOPE

When summer is back,
and the sun shines so bright,
our faces light up
and our hearts are cheered up
by the sight.
It seems so strange,
that, now, we're caught,
we doubt ourselves,

our memories of winter days,
and even our ways of thought.
Are these our friends?
Is this the same place?
So, our greenness,
when faced with grey
its pigment young
could not ferment.
Our strength, our life,
so young and pure,
without the sun,
had lost its face.
The restless in our soul,
in youthful urge to spend itself,
sought to drown
in emptiness.
That each thrill and each excitement,
seemed to bear, in plates of gold,
the joy and peace
we, never, owned.
But time is come
when we must fold
our winters gone
as histories old.
Let us go, and with a song
And live and love
with the kindly sun.

NOT TO BE

Your love was perfect
in its half.
My half, its wisdom

never serves.

A union short
and of two
helps achieve
our life's to do.

Sins can glitter.
Hades can shine.
With ourselves
they have no chance.

Matchless beauties,
so, we were.
Ancient blood
of proud degree.

Jealous hearts,
died in vain.
Gentle hearts,
wished us well.

Peace was ours
by our pact.
Soul and body
came as one.

But who has heard
of such a thing?
Or seen a heaven
here on earth?

Follies, follies,

18

so, unleashed
Must shine twice
to blind the eyes.

Try the tongue,
it must be tied.
Try the brain,
it must be dead.

Such a treat
is not for us.
Such a bliss
is not to be.

THE THINGS WE LOST

At times like these we pay our dues
and sit around and cry like little kids.
And those things which meant nothing before our eyes
reveal their beauty and haunt our desires.
And our seconds of brave and resourceful fights,
spread in years of waste before our awakening sights
and what we had and manipulated in our grip,
when our eyes refused and would not even see.
escape and vow never to be our own again.
That their absence opens our eyes
and fills the heart with pain.
What happened to these hands, and to these eyes?
Or were these senses tired or dead with sleep?
The heart was keen and prayed for peace.
The body tried its best and did its share.
Was the soul not full of virtue?
Or the brain of thoughts that serve?

Why this, then? Why this loss?

NOT FOR ME

Like a man in darkness born
I, often, have to try to fight,
when, like a shadow, quick to form,
light would dawn and dazzle the sight.
For though, in light, there is life.
Yet, it's not for me to bathe
But for them that can let be.
And that I cannot ever do.
No. Life? Not for me.

BIGOTS

Tentacles in search for peace,
ever, ever at their reach,
are numbed and burnt in times like these,
by men as such as these.

All the smarting we suppress,
all the wrath and passion boiled,
all are stirred and stoked by them.
Not knowing, really, what they do.

If we did not know them well,
their soul's frustration in a veil.
If we placed their ways of thought
on the planes on which they stand,

If we had not trained before,
by much experience that is past,

to smart and sigh in place of war,
can they survive the way they are?

If we did not know before
to rule the ego, fancy prone,
with reason tried and furnace true,
then this peace, this brotherhood
which you claim are much in need
has not a hope and not a friend.

All the things we ever learnt,
all the virtues, its ethic,
all the pains we bore to learn,
now, to naught, will go in vain
and just be effort made in vain.

All, alike, will join and fight,
the blood of war to shed and drink
whose taste and flavour, in its filth
will teach to all the sense of it
that love and peace are best.

THE INNOCENT OPPRESSED

If the skies were known to me,
the silvery moon would soothe.
If all spite and sorrows die
I would have them tried.

If all galaxies and their stars
inspired me to ride
and riding have your wonders mine,
you can keep your world.

I will go and leave you here
to stay and reap of what you sow.
Your ways alone can please its mien
and force its service on your wont.

It serves not the tender ways.
Its ends justify its means.
For though it sings in decency,
it cares not just one bean.

REFLECTIONS

At the dawn of the night,
when the day is done,
our sorrows, as if of right,
come to put us down.
In our lives, a look around
keeps us mute,
as we see and feel again
the long-forgotten sights.
Our dreams are pale.
Our hopes, our pride,
have gone to Hades

AFTER

GROW UP, MAN

Grow up, man! Grow up, man!
Look around you! Look around!
Faith? Ha! Ha! Look again.
Whoever keeps it must want to die.

Love? Ha! Ha! Come again.
Can't you see? Are you blind?
It's not pure. It's not true.
All is fair in love and war.

Morals? Ha! Justice? Boo!
Caring? That's for fools.
One love? Dear, you must be mad.
Chastity? Boy, you're green.

Grow up, man! Grow up, man!
Take some time
to grow up, man.

I WILL BELIEVE IN GOD

I will believe in this your God
but need my dolls to stay alive.
I will believe in this one God
to spruce my speech at any time.
I will believe in many gods
so, your own needs me not.
I will believe in any god
or dad and mum will be annoyed.
I will believe in God the Good
but deal with hate I must address.

25

I will believe in this your God
who lets me be to create in play.
I will believe in any god
because a man must find *wackies*.
I will believe in any god
who lets me smirk about the things
which Jane and John are said to do,
even though I do the same.
I will believe in this your God
because He lets me look and see
when common Jim will better me.
I will believe in any god
who blames me not for Peter's wife;
a pure delight you, never, saw;
and willing, joyful too.
I will believe in this your God
who lets us do what we would like.
I'd like to swear I do believe.
But you and I; we know quite well
nobody, really, does believe.

I KNOW A GIRL

I know a girl who tells me lies.
I search her face; she tells me mine.
I seek her eyes, she captures mine.
She looks so hard I change my gaze.

I used to think - I heard so too -
a look, a liar's face would pull.
It used to be that just a stare
would make a liar ill at ease.

26

But now, I hear that all of that
is just an act, a simple act.
A mirror, practice, shift of mind,
and who is he to stand your stare?

While you tell and when you like
all the lies that you can tell.

CUCKOLD

The chest goes tight, the insides dry;
all the signs of death are there,
when you hear of Chaucer's tales
and read that called *The Miller's Tale*.

You dare not check. You dare not think
of things your eyes can see or take.
Yet, you cannot wish away
things that look like they must be.

You try to plead and then, to swear,
or lick the grime to bear the tears.
But you will find, for all your pain,
that new evils gain.

You dare complain, you get ignored.
You dare demand, you get the tongue.
All the friends and foes you have
will come and swear that you have cracked.

Proud they are these grown up kids.
Sure, they are of mastery.
They must be sure of fiends that guide

their luck, their nerve, their tongue.

What is more, they think it ripe
to deal with you, you boring bore.
With demons working overtime,
they'd show you, just to kill your soul,
more adult games.

MR. GOODMAN

I am a good man, very good man;
and that is why I die.
What is due I give to all
though, nobody, ever, gives me mine.

I labour so much not to hurt.
but, every time, they want me hurt.
Resent I do when gossip flies.
hear you too when, thus, maligned.

But me, I'm smeared without an end
and tarred without a thought or word.
Nothing done is, ever, strange.
Naught beyond my won't to do.

Lies to tell I do abhor.
but me, I'm lied to all the time.
To cheat I'd fly and rather die.
But me, to cheat, they rush and vie.

I'd rather faint, that extra mile,
to avoid deceit of friend or foe.
But everyone I meet to know

deceives me, just a matter of time.

The whole of me I make to give
in friendliness and all I have.
But see the gift I, always, get
to show that they resent my best.

All I have I give in love.
But I receive in bowls of hate.
Only my friends, in this our life,
have problems, not me. How can I?

My friends, alone, are ill, not I.
My friends, alone, are, ever, broke.
My friends, alone, have work to do.
And all I have is idle time.

When I'm dead, I'm sure to hear
how my friends will ask, in pain,
why I could not come to share
all the pain they bear in vain.

What kind of friend, they'd ask, am I
who cannot come to aid his friends?
And this is just to come and mix
and then, be lost amidst their crowd.

See? Don't you? Just my fault.
I did not wake and rise, though dead,
to give their honour to my friends.
See? Don't you? It's all my fault.
I'm not a good man, not at all.

VOX POPULI, REVISITED

Tonight, in my nights,
today, in my days,
my heart weighs down
to ensure that I'm down.

They said it'll be so.
They said I'd better know.
But me, I thought I'd go
against what they know.

You see? They are judge.
You see? They are wrong.
When everybody ought
nobody, ever, judge.

How was I to know
that they were right?
And everybody knows
that we should be wise.

FOREIGN CHARM

Sheila N, Julie N,
Sonya, Freda, Mary N.
Single name, double name.
Both of them would be the same.

Had I not, myself, in arms,
to scare and run from foreign charm,
then, my tongue would not have stuck
when, in chance, we met our love.

Now, I find my fears in vain.
Now, in years, I look again.
I see your smile and lovely face.
And wish that I had had the grace.

LOVE LOST

When you find yourself in love,
do not, ever, ever, slip.
When you find you're, greatly, loved,
do not, ever, ever, scheme.

How can you destroy a love,
when you know not what could be?
How can you believe in love,
and strive to kill the love you see?

Raise a cry. Shed a tear.
How can you awake the dead?
Break your heart. Tear your hair.
What has gone, has gone, is dead.

See me in my reverie.
See me in my misery.
Tell me she is near not far.
Tell me we can mend our past.

NIGHTMARE SPOUSE

Misfortune
can come too soon.
Disaster
is made to star,

when your spouse,
a nightmare spouse.

All the don'ts,
your spouse is wont.
All your pride
will be to ride,
for those of them
that dared not dare.

Give your love
in search of love.
Sacrifice
in peace device.
What a stool
for spouse's foot!

Try and pause,
you find you curse.
Bear and wait,
your name they paint,
stupid, blind bat,
cuckold mat.

This must end -
you seek the end.
Seek the truth,
you swear forsooth.
Your friends, your mates,
you find are fakes.

So, you swear
to kill or bear.

Both of which
will cure no itch.

Then, you see
that you must grouse
through life's sea
with nightmare spouse.

EVIL IN TOWN

There's an evil in this town;
an evil that is fueled by all.
Two pairs of legs will play the game,
when hid, without a pride or shame.

It was a good, an act of God,
to make paradise, God's great love,
to use the power of His love
to make His work a thing of joy.

But now, I know it's not the same.
For, what I see I bow in shame.
Husbands, wives, and kids galore
have joined the fray in this our town.

You think your wife is not in it.
For sure, your husband? No such thing!
Your sons and daughters, how can they?
But then, you're hit by things you see.

They say they're going to work or school,
to shop, to post, to bank or so.
But what they've, really, gone to do

33

is meet with them you'll never know.

You ask and ask and get abused.
Kobo stamps and cheques that bounce,
Condiments for soup, and rice
take all day to find and buy?

You task yourself and check the norm,
and find that custom, church, and law,
in one voice and that is sure,
says it's evil, true and clear.

You raise a cry on this premise
and call on custom, old, and wise.
The shock will kill you but for shame
when you find it's all a game.

Then, you hope to bank on friends.
and find dismay. They are afraid.
Do not judge or else be judged.
Put asunder - face the Judge.

You rush to church, it's God's own house,
and they will hear and give advice.
This is life, you'll hear them say,
you've got to bear and pray and pray.

Oh! No! You swear. I'll use the law,
where you know they, still, will know.
But nobody wants to use the law.
It's fair. It's square. It is a show.

34

So, you see this evil thing
that Satan, now, has put in town,
we can't remove without a fight,
Without our God and His support.

HIS UGLINESS

I met him once.
I saw him twice.
I know him now
quite in and out.

His head is big.
His eyes are large.
His ears, his lips,
his tongue, are flags

A skin like rhino's
old and gone,
with folds and spots
the kinds we see
on reptiles, which
I loathe to name.

It makes you wonder
why on earth
a creature such
will be a man,
with ugliness
so real and true.

But that's the point -
just ugliness.

And nothing but
his ugliness

His ugliness is everywhere
in everything he says and does.
But me, I think the worst is this
the things he does with people's wives.

I found out, too, his specialty.
His kind, the wives of good young men
who slave and work and too busy,
to see or think the things they do.

I know he's bad and knows his kind,
these demons true who pose as wives,
who catch and tie with vicious nerve,
good young men who wish to serve.

How they meet I do not know.
How he woos them is his trade.
But this I know, they'll kill their spouse
just to meet His Ugliness.

MALAISE

The skies may wait
if they can.
The moon can shine
if it wants.
The sun will have to shine
or there's no day.
And the stars?
They're so far,

farther, even, than the moon and sun,
that I dare not
put my trust in them.
What have they to do
with my soul?
What can they say
about my pain?
Do they care
if I'm sick?
Or weep
when I die?
Let them be.
They cannot help.

JUST MY LIFE (BRAIN DRAIN?)

Wuthering Heights of English lore,
scraggy peaks and snowy caps,
mountain faces, sheer and low,
from Ben Nevis to the Alps,
have chased away our rounded hills.

Our green verdure and hot terrains,
with storms and thunders and their rains,
our floods and torrents, with their slopes,
our snakes and tigers, antelopes,
have run before their tender sheep.

Their healthy cows, with so much milk,
with cheese and joints and rounded chucks,
have made our rhinos and our crocs,
our goats and chimps and all their ilk,
things vexatious, tedious jobs.

I hear you moan about my deed
without one thought about my need.
Where were you, my friend indeed?
When in love with rounded hills,
I went to enjoy the green verdure.

I sought the sun to warm my bones.
I thought the fruits were good and due.
I saw the brook to cool my domes.
But I was bitten by the snake.
And chased by tigers on the take.

The rhinos thought me very much game.
All the insects bit the same.
The crocs would not, even, let me know.
It's just by luck that I was saved
by their seasons and their snow.

I looked around and found out too.
Their snakes are pets and do not bite.
Their tigers, lions, live in zoos.
Why, my friend, the ballyhoo?
Brain Drain? No. It's just my life!

KNOW YOUR SIDE

Satan is the father of lies;
do you know his sons?
Satan, now, ahead, and wise,
have his daughters put you on?

If you are a child of God
can you tell His ways?

If you play in the team of God
can you tell your mates?

When your mate is battle joined,
ringed by demons and their lies,
to shame and club to break his joints.
do their tricks your hands all tie?

When your mate, by them, oppressed,
fights and fights, there seems no end.
When he calls in his distress
in whose team are you, my friend?

How you see and hear and judge:
these are things for Satan's ploy.
What can make his works prosper
than God's team members' thoughtless props?

That though you like to call on God,
you serve the demons by your bond
to sentiments and laziness
and things you hear and don't reflect.

So, wake up now and chose your side.
If you choose the side of God,
know the things your side is for,
and fight, committed, to His side.

EMPTY SPOUSES

I know a husband and his wife.
I know a husband with no wife.
I know a wife who lost her man.

I know them all and all their plans.

I heard, before, the spouse is dear,
your friend, your love, your confidant.
Your fears, your hopes, your secret thoughts
are known and shared by you alone.

But now, I hear the genuine spouse
is blank and shallow, stonewall like.
And all her friends are her secrets,
with all the things they do or share.

I have my fears, my secret fears.
I have my tastes, those childish joys.
I have, sometimes, I fall in love.
You do not think I'll tell my spouse.

A lovely spouse is there for peace.
What peace is there if my spouse should know?
I know this peace is devil's peace.
But that's the one the world would own.

That, now, the spouse will swear in fiat:
"I do not cheat my spouse in faith.
To give my love and all my laugh,
why, my friend! I'll be a mat!"

With all of this, they fret and try
to find a way to bear their life,
not knowing, really, what they are
empty spouses here and there.

THE RIGHT APPROACH

Hurrah! I've found the right approach!
I'll talk. I'll do. I'll drink my fill.
I'll take and cheat and lie and kill.
For these are things that go with it,
when you have the right approach.

The years I worked! In vain I toiled
to help my friends and foes alike.
I sought the good of all I met,
but all it did was bring regret.
You see? I lacked the right approach.

When you have the right approach,
you'll know the time to play the hurt.
You'll know the time to be a sport,
to give no gifts or do a turn.
And, still, they'll think you're lots of fun.

You'll learn to tap the ego talk
and use the ear to free the tongue.
In all your talk, no right or wrong,
no thief, condemned, will bear your talk.
And this is true in right approach.

You get to learn and act it too,
that people living, bad and good,
do not care to think or check
the things you say or do or fake,
so long as you will ride their horse.

The good and bad, alike, you'll find

41

will die for you or sell their kind,
for things they loathe and hate like hell.
And when for you, they'd rush to hell,
There! You've got the right approach.

AN ARMY MAN

I am just an army man;
on land and sea and air, I am.
They got me dressed in their khakis
and made me wear their special caps.

I learnt some books, they turn me sour,
your schools are full of sobering thoughts.
No life for me, I have my plan.
I'll take the gun and be a man.

My life is rich and full of flair,
with marching, singing, healthy air.
We drill and drill to go to war,
although I've never been to one.

I do complain, in time, sometimes,
but this, I know, is part of life.
I am happy with myself,
with God, with life, with everything.

I did not care, I did not fret,
till you woke me with your noise.
Why must I be stressed yet dumb?
While my country burns.

How can I, with all my guns,

stand and watch and not be stung,
while the learned and the wise,
treat, as farce, our fate, our life?

The pests I'll chase away at once
and shoot them who won't want to run.
I'll show them how our things are done
and what will make our lives a song.

But wait! I think I've found the hitch
why our wise cannot agree.
The loot is much and no restraints,
I'll help myself and all my friends.

I'm not worse, than them wise rats.
I do not jar or strain your nerves.
I do not make you fight yourselves.
I do not take to flaunt as wealth.

So, you see? The army man,
with guns and bluff and all of it,
has more to him than you can think.
So? Get yourself an army man!

EMPOWERED GAL

I met a girl, a lovely girl
who learnt some books and rides a car.
She has a man and has some kids.
She has a job as high and new.

I'll tell you, now, the things she said.
I'll tell you some but not the rest,

Because I do not have the head
to know them all she said to me.

"I am a gal, empowered gal.
I learnt some books, have keys and car.
I'll match a man in anything
with more can-do than he can think.

I see my youth. I know it well.
I saw my mum with all her chores.
I saw my dad with all his chums,
in wrappers, singlet, snuff, and wine.

They went out early, came back late,
and sat to chat and share their jokes,
while my mum, from morn till late,
bore the heat, the stench, the smoke.

I asked my mum the reason why.
And all she said was, "they are men,
and we, the women, we must work
to keep our homes for you and them".

Now, I'm grown. My eyes are wide.
And been-to, been-from, yes, I am.
And all that tale of child and men,
see me? Stuff it here and there!

I know this life. It is so short.
It can be sweet. It can be hot.
It's up to you, if you may ask,
to make it nice or arduous task.

The choice, for me, is just as clear
As daylight, and from year to year.
To pick my joys and pleasures now,
not minding what you think or how.

I hear the kids have gone berserk
and steal and rob and life forsake.
I hear that homes are nothing much,
with dad and mum not being around.

I'm sure it's me you think should stay
to bear and wear like good old mum,
while my man will have his way
with girls as young or old as mum.

A gal can do what man can do,
and better, even, than they boast.
What? With all the tricks I know.
Why? My friend let's hear the rest!

I hear you talk of hell below,
and all of them that there would go.
You talk of heaven and its joys.
But you and I may get a shock.

Methinks that heaven, all that talk,
is just a tale to keep in check,
the ways a gal may want to walk,
to make men, always, top the scale".

Tell me now, my friend, my man
what to do with all these gals.
Do we agree that they are right?

45

Do we fight to save our lives?

KNIFE EDGE FRIENDS

I saw a knife with two sharp sides;
an edge apiece, a two-edged knife.
I saw it sharp and cutting prone.
I bought it, fast, to make my own.

I know a knife, inanimate.
I know, a slip, it cuts you eight.
Yet, a knife I know at night.
A knife, I'm sure, has not a heart.

I have my friends, there's many here.
See us play, you'll drop a tear
and wish that all your life, on earth,
is filled with friends as good as them.

I have to say, and that may shock,
that I will rather take the knives
than have these friends that fill your stock
who breathe and talk but cut like knives.

INDEX OF FIRST LINES

www.ingramcontent.com/pod-product-compliance
Lightning Source LLC
Chambersburg PA
CBHW070830100426
42813CB00003B/565